P9-DLZ-371

PRAYING MANTISES

A TRUE BOOK

by

Larry Dane Brimner

Children's Press®
A Division of Grolier Publishing
New York London Hong Kong Sydney
Danbury, Connecticut

A deadleaf mantid
with its wings spread

Subject Consultant
Jeffrey Hahn
Associate Professor
University of Minnesota
Extension Service
Department of Entomology

Reading Consultant
Linda Cornwell
Coordinator of School Quality
and Professional Improvement
Indiana State Teachers
Association

Dedication:
For kids everywhere
who love bugs

Visit Children's Press® on
the Internet at:
http://publishing.grolier.com

The cover photo shows a
bordered mantid. The title-
page photo shows a praying
mantis eating a grasshopper.

Library of Congress Cataloging-in-Publication Data

Brimner, Larry Dane.
Praying mantises / Larry Dane Brimner.
      p.   cm. — (A true book)
    Includes bibliographical references (p.) and index.
    Summary: Describes the physical characteristics, behavior, life cycle,
protective devices, and relatives of the praying mantis.
    ISBN 0-516-21163-3 (lib.bdg.)   0-516-26769-8 (pbk.)
1. Praying mantis—Juvenile literature.   [1. Praying mantis.] I. Title. II.
Series.
QL508.M4B75   1999
595.7'27—dc21   99-13837
                                                                                      CIP
                                                                                      AC

GROLIER
PUBLISHING   1 2 3 4 5 6 7 8 9 10 R 08 07 06 05 04 03 02 01 00 99

Contents

The Hunter   5

Saying its Prayers   10

Relatives or Not   24

Danger!   28

A Cozy Place for Eggs   32

From Nymphs to Adults   36

To Find Out More   44

Important Words   46

Index   47

Meet the Author   48

A praying mantis
about to catch a
grasshopper

The Hunter

A praying mantis is perched on a stem near a flower. It is hunting for a meal. The mantis's green color blends in well with the surrounding leaves and twigs. This protects the mantis from birds, bats, and other animals that might want to eat it. It also helps the mantis catch

its prey. It eats other insects
and, sometimes, small tree
frogs.

A butterfly stops at a flower
to drink nectar. It does not see
the mantis waiting nearby. The
mantis stays perfectly still—it
is a patient hunter. It waits for

just the right moment. Then the mantis strikes out with its spiny front legs and snatches the butterfly. It strikes so fast that human eyes cannot detect it.

A praying mantis eating a moth

Now the mantis eats the wriggling meal it holds in its powerful front legs.

Mantises eat only live prey. If it drops part of the butterfly, the mantis will not pick it up.

Praying mantises have powerful front legs.

After it eats, the praying mantis grooms itself almost like a cat. It cleans its front legs. Then it uses first one front leg, then the other, to clean every part of its head. Clean eyes and its antennae, or feelers, will help it find another meal.

Saying its Prayers

A praying mantis is like other insects in many ways. Its body is divided into three parts—the head, the thorax, and the abdomen. It has six legs and two large compound eyes. These eyes are made up of thousands of lenses, or facets. Each lens is like a

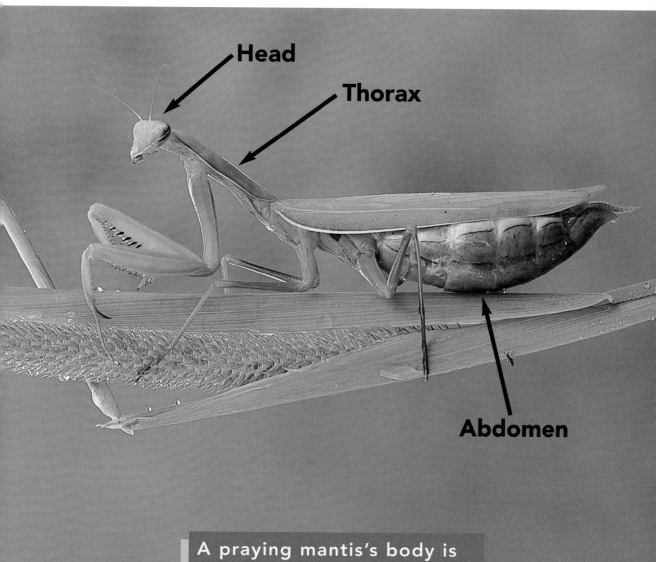

Head

Thorax

Abdomen

A praying mantis's body is divided into three parts: head, thorax, and abdomen.

A close-up view of a praying mantis's eyes

separate eye. A tough outer shell, called an exoskeleton, protects the mantis's body like a suit of armor.

But praying mantises are different from other insects in

some ways. A praying mantis can turn its triangular head over its shoulders to see its prey—and its enemies. If you walk past a mantis, it will turn its head to watch you. No other insect can do this!

A praying mantis can turn its head to look at you!

Its sharp mouthparts are made for chewing live prey, and its two long, thin antennae help it find food.

A praying mantis's mouth is made for chewing live prey (above). Praying mantises have two long antennae (right).

Praying mantises have three pairs of legs and two pairs of wings.

The legs and wings of a mantis are attached to the thorax. A mantis has three pairs

The front pair of legs has spines and hooks.

of legs. The front pair has spines and hooks that catch and hold prey. A mantis usually folds these legs as if it were saying its prayers. This is why

A mantis in the "praying" pose

people call it a "praying man-tis." The other two pairs of legs are used for moving around on twigs and branches.

Mantises
spread their
wings when
threatened.

Usually, mantises move slowly. They hunt by waiting and watching patiently for prey to come to them. Mantises can fly, but they also spread their wings to frighten away enemies.

Many kinds of mantises also have a slit on the underside of the thorax. This is the mantis's ear. Scientists believe that mantises are the only animals with just one ear.

When a mantis is in flight, this special ear tells it if bats are nearby. The minute a mantis hears a bat, it flies in the opposite direction to avoid being captured.

The abdomen of the mantis has several segments, or parts. The male mantis, which is usually smaller than the female, has eight segments in its abdomen. The female has only six. The female also has a tube called an ovipositor for laying eggs.

The male mantis is smaller than the female mantis.

Hiding in the Open

Bordered mantis

Praying mantises have various ways of protecting themselves. One way is by using camouflage. They blend in with their surroundings.

Tree-bark mantis

Stick mantis

Their color and thin bodies make them hard to see. Some types of mantises look like green twigs. Others look like bark or dead leaves. One of the rarest is the Asian orchid mantis. It blends in with pink tropical flowers.

Dead-leaf mantis

Orchid mantis

Leaf mantis

Relatives or Not?

Entomologists—scientists who study insects—call mantises mantids. They say that there are about 1,800 different kinds of mantids in the world. Most of them live in warmer climates, but a few kinds are found in colder places. Some entomologists say praying mantises are

Kikori giant praying mantis, New Guinea

Orchid mantis, Malaysia

European mantid

Chinese mantid

Carolina mantid

related to cockroaches. Others say they are more like grasshoppers and crickets. But most scientists now agree that mantids make up a group of their own.

Three kinds of praying mantises are common to North America: the European mantid, the Chinese mantid, and the Carolina mantid. The Carolina mantid is native to North America. The others probably arrived along with the cargo in a ship. No one knows for sure.

Danger!

By late summer, the abdomen
of a female praying mantis is
full of eggs. She is ready to
have a family, but she needs a
male to help her. Scientists
think female mantises produce
a chemical that attracts males.
A male mantis senses this
chemical and knows the female

A female mantis with an abdomen full of eggs

will welcome him. The male then spreads his wings wide and curls up his abdomen to

A male and female praying mantis getting ready to mate

get the female's attention. If the female likes what she sees, she holds out her front legs. Scientists think this is a signal that lets the male know she will not harm him.

After they mate, the male takes off with a flying leap. For the male mantis, there is danger in mating. Usually, he does not leap far enough away, and the female eats him!

The female mantis often eats the male after mating.

A Cozy Place for Eggs

Now the female mantis must find a safe place to lay her eggs. She usually chooses a stem or branch well above the ground. She then hangs upside down, and foam begins to flow from the end of her abdomen. Her abdomen moves in circles to form an

A female mantis
creating an ootheca

33

The ootheca
is filled with
hundreds of
eggs.

egg case, called an ootheca, out of the foam.

The egg case is about the size of a walnut. It hardens quickly and makes a cozy home for one hundred to three hundred eggs. The female mantis makes several such egg cases before winter comes.

A female mantis does not raise her young. In fact, she never meets them. Once she has laid her eggs, her work is done. She will not live much longer.

From Nymphs to Adults

In spring, the weather begins to warm up. Soon, hundreds of tiny praying mantises push through slits in the bottom of the egg case. These young mantises, called nymphs, are no bigger than mosquitoes. They wriggle out of the sacs that protected them as they

Nymphs emerging
from the egg case

The nymphs dangle down to the ground from thin, white threads.

grew inside the egg case.
Then they dangle down from
thin, white threads to the
ground, and hurry for shelter.

Nymphs look like tiny versions of their parents. The only difference is that nymphs do not have fully formed wings.

Right after a nymph hatches, its hard skin—the exoskeleton—is already feeling tight.

Nymphs are much tinier than adult mantises.

So the nymph sheds it in order to grow. This is called molting. The nymph hangs upside down from a twig or stem. It splits open its old skin and wriggles free. In a few hours, its new skin hardens into a new exoskeleton. Now the nymph is ready for life on its own—and ready for its first meal.

A young mantis is born knowing how to survive. Its front legs are ready to catch

Growing, Growing, Grown

As a nymph grows larger and larger, its exoskeleton remains the same size. Each time the exoskeleton gets too tight, the nymph molts. A nymph goes through six to nine molts before becoming an adult. The last time it slips out of its tight skin, it will have fully formed wings.

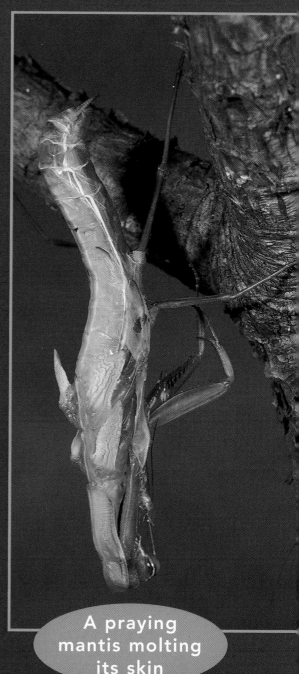

A praying mantis molting its skin

A mantis nymph

and hold its prey. Its sharp
mouthparts are ready to bite and
chew. Before their first day is
done, some mantises will eat
other nymphs—alive—to survive!
By fall, the nymphs will be ready
to have babies of their own.

We may find some things about praying mantises disturbing—their looks or their habit of eating each other. But for all their unusual habits, these backyard hunters are part of nature's careful balance.

To Find Out More

Here are some additional resources to help you learn more about praying mantises:

Books

Lavies, Bianca. **Backyard Hunter: The Praying Mantis.** Puffin Unicorn Books, 1990.

Russo, Monica. **Insect Almanac: A Year-Round Activity Guide.** Sterling Publishing, 1991.

Stefoff, Rebecca. **Praying Mantis.** Benchmark Books, 1997.

Watts, Barrie. **Stick Insects.** Franklin Watts, 1991.

Organizations and Online Sites

Bug Club
http://www.ex.ac.uk/ bugclub/

The webpage of the Amateur Entomologists' Society's Bug Club for Young Entomologists, a British club devoted to young people who are fascinated by bugs. It provides a newsletter, lists club events, and includes a page on how to keep praying mantises as pets.

Get this Bug off of Me!
http://www.uky.edu/ Agriculture/Entomology/ ythfacts/hurtrnot.htm

This site, sponsored by the University of Kentucky, describes common insects—including praying mantises—that, though scary-looking, don't hurt humans.

Virtual Insectary
http://www.vt.edu:10021/ forestry/wildlife/stein/ insects.html

Provides images of some common insects—including praying mantises—and includes information on their habitats and the foods they eat.

Young Entomologists' Society, Inc.
6907 West Grand River Avenue
Lansing, MI 48906
http://insects.ummz./lsa. umich.edu/YES/YES.html

An organization that provides publications and outreach programs for young people interested in insect study.

Important Words

camouflage any disguise that hides or protects

compound eye eye that has many lenses

entomologist scientist who studies insects

lens part of the eye that focuses rays of light so as to form clear images

molt to shed the outer skin

ootheca egg case

ovipositor organ on an insect used for depositing eggs

nymphs the young of certain types of insects; they differ from the adult insect in that they are smaller and do not have fully developed wings

prey animal that is hunted by another animal for food

threatened made to feel in danger

Index

(**Boldface** page numbers indicate illustrations.)

abdomen, 10, **11**, 20, 28, 32
antennae, 9, 14, **14**
Asian orchid mantis, 23, **23, 25**
bats, 5, 20
birds, 5
bordered mantid, **cover, 22**
camouflage, 22
Carolina mantid, **26**, 27
Chinese mantid, **26**, 27
deadleaf mantid, **2, 23**
cockroaches, 27
compound eyes, 10
crickets, 27
ear, 19, 20
egg case, **34**, 35, 36, **37, 38**
eggs, 28, **29**, 32, **34**, 35
entomologists, 24
European mantid, **26**, 27
exoskeleton, 12, 39, 40, 41, **41**
eyes, 12, **12**

female mantis, 20, **21**, 28, **29**, 30, **30**, 31, **31**, 32, **33**
grasshoppers, 1, **4**, 27
grooming, 9, **9**
head, 10, **11**, 13, **13**
Kikori giant praying mantis, **25**
leaf mantis, **23**
legs, 7, 8, **8**, 10, 15, **15**, 16, **16**, 17
male mantis, 20, **21**, 28, 29, 30, **30**, 31, **31**
molting, 40, 41, **41**
mouthparts, 14, **14**, 42
North America, 27
nymphs, 36, **37, 38**, 39, **39**, 40, 41, 42, **42**
ootheca, **33, 34**, 35, **37**
ovipositor, 20
"praying" pose, 17, **17**
prey, 6, 8, 13, 14, 16, 19, 42
stick mantis, **22**
thorax, 10, **11**, 15, 19
tree-bark mantis, **22**
tree frogs, 6
wings, 15, **15, 18**, 19, 41

Meet the Author

Larry Dane Brimner is a former teacher who now writes full-time for children. The author of more than sixty books, his previous Children's Press titles include *The Winter Olympics, Bobsledding and the Luge,* and a series of books about the planets. When he isn't writing, Larry visits with children in schools across the United States to discuss the writing process.

AAW-1815